THE RETURN ROOM

D1420480

W.R. Rodgers by Sidney Smith, 1941

THE RETURN ROOM

W.R. RODGERS

Illustrations by

GERARD DILLON

The idea for the publication of *The Return Room* came to me almost twenty years ago when BBC producer, Douglas Carson, found the lost recording of the 1955 production in the BBC Northern Ireland archives. It has taken time and changes in recording technology to bring together the elements of this publication: the printed script; the compact disc; Gerard Dillon's illustrations; Paul Muldoon's foreword; and Douglas Carson's introduction. The programme illustrates the Rodgers technique which Patric Stevenson described as conveying a 'pawky sense of humour [that] flashes delightfully now and [. . .

I am grat[...] sister, Dr Nini [...] Dillon (the Gera[...]Estate), Patsy H[...]Gillian McIntos[...]Myron Cohen, f[...]

First published in 2010 by
Blackstaff Press
4c Heron Wharf, Sydenham Business Park
Belfast BT3 9LE
with the assistance of
The Arts Council of Northern Ireland

arts
council
of Northern Ireland

Design by Dunbar Design
Printed in County Antrim by W. & G. Baird

A CIP catalogue record for this book
is available from the British Library

ISBN 978-0-85640-861-8

www.blackstaffpress.com

CONTENTS

W.R. Rodgers in the manse, Loughgall

FOREWORD

PAUL MULDOON

I have no hesitation in describing *The Return Room* as one of the most important Irish poems of the twentieth century, allowing no less insight into the Irish society of its moment than Patrick Kavanagh's *The Great Hunger* or Derek Mahon's 'A Disused Shed in County Wexford'.

Some may balk at my description of *The Return Room* as a poem. I suggest that its very title is based on two key notions of poetry making. The idea of 'return' is central to the business of versification. As it happens, an astonishingly high percentage of *The Return Room* is written in verse, much of it drawn from the popular song and street-rhyme traditions. The word 'room' is yet another pointer to Rodgers's artistic ambition, translating as it does one sense of the word 'stanza'.

The chamber of *The Return Room* is an exceptionally capacious one, partly because it's 'a dead-end room, kept for visitors'. It's part lumber room, in other words, part living museum. I stress the word 'living', because one of the ongoing strengths of this poem is its unerring sense of the essential imagery of the Belfast experience, not only in 1915 or 1955 but also in 2015. It's as if one were presented with the grave goods of a nation, a mini-version of Sutton Hoo or Broighter, and encouraged to extrapolate the core of the national being:

Holy Mary, Mother of God,
Pray for me and Tommy Todd:
Tommy Todd is a Prod,
Holy Mary, Mother of God.

Such a quatrain goes to the heart of the Belfast experience, with a directness coupled with a devilish delight from which many would now feel obliged to shy away. What I love about *The Return Room* is the cherishing of the very stereotypes we're now generally required to suppress. My strong belief is that the sooner we feel comfortable again with the public presentation of lines like 'Tommy Todd is a Prod,/ Holy Mary, Mother of God' the better off we'll all be. Northern Ireland needs a bit of political incorrectness, which is not to say we need to return to Unionist misrule.

To get back to *The Return Room* as a poem, we can only marvel at it as 'a piece of structural engineering', a poem being just that – no less riveting, or *riveted*, than anything launched from the shipyards. As a technical feat, it represents the highest form of artistic achievement. The combination of sound effects of the 'Island horn' with a three-headed narration allows for a multiplicity of perspectives:

> Mrs Mulligan, a mile away, crossed herself uneasily as the Protestant
> feet tramped past her house. And her twelve children fell quiet under
> the bedclothes for fear the feet might quicken and break into a run.

The narrative of the Mulligan family is only one to which Rodgers would come back at regular intervals in the way that stabilisers and ballast tanks are incorporated at regular intervals into the hull of a ship. Even if one may trace W. R. Rodgers's working method to a number of antecedents – the generic radio feature as it had been developed by the BBC, the specific example of Dylan Thomas's *Under Milk Wood*, the punsterism of James Joyce in *Finnegans Wake*, the verbal high jinks of his own more conventional verse – it's clear that, in *The Return Room*, he had laid down the keel of a vessel only he was equipped to build:

> Son of Adam; Sin of Adam,
> I was the heir to all that Adamnation
> And hand-me-down of doom; the old newcomer
> To the return room.

An indicator of Rodgers's achievement, I suggest, is the fact that, like *The Great Hunger* and 'A Disused Shed in County Wexford,'

The Return Room is at once wholly influential and wholly inimitable, that it manages, in a quite unexpected way, to 'lead nowhere and back again'. Its very particular combination of regard for ritual and complete irreverence, joined like the Orange and the Green 'in holy deadlock', has given it an irrefutable place in the canon.

When I worked for the BBC in Belfast, between 1974 and 1986, *The Return Room* was already held up as an example of radio at its peak. Many of those involved in the programme – Bill Hunter, J.G. Devlin, Catherine Gibson, Sam Hanna Bell – were still going strong and helping producers like myself find the truth in Louis MacNeice's observation that 'sound can do many fine things which will never be possible on television'.

There were still tales of how the Lambeg drum player, who had been stationed on the roof of Broadcasting House with a cue light to alert him to when he should start playing, wasn't given a cue to let him know when he should stop. It was only when the live broadcast was over and the rest of the production team of *The Return Room* were leaving the building for a drink that they realised the drummer was still going strong. I think of the drummer at his drum as an image for the persistence of art.

The Return Room belongs to that very particular strand of oral poetry that grants us a broad and deep sense of a 'city of ships and shawlies, doles and doyleys' which might otherwise be only imperfectly conveyed by thousands of pages of conventional history, conventional geography, conventional sociology, and conventional psychology.

W.R. Rodgers by Rowel Friers, *c.* 1955

INTRODUCTION

DOUGLAS CARSON

The Return Room *was the finest radio feature produced in Northern Ireland after the Second World War. It was an evocation of a writer's boyhood in Ulster. This introduction describes how it came to be made.*

In January 1952, the Belfast papers carried a brief death notice:

RODGERS
At her residence, 39 The Mount,
Jane Ferris, wife of Robert S. Rodgers.
House and funeral private.

Jane Ferris Rodgers was the mother of the poet, W.R. Rodgers. Her departure cut his links with Mountpottinger in east Belfast, where he grew up. His father was nearly a hundred years old: he moved to the Isle of Man, and the home passed to others.

In 1953, the poet's wife, Marie Waddell, died. Soon afterwards, he married Marianne Helweg. She was the former wife of Laurence Gilliam, Head of the BBC Features Department. They went to live in Stoke-by-Nayland, Essex, and Rodgers looked for work as a writer and broadcaster. He was forty-four.

On 1 October, his father, Robert Skelly Rodgers, 'retired insurance agent', died at Nobles Hospital, Douglas. He was buried in Kirk Bradden Cemetery on the Isle of Man.

They are gone, the old residenters. The mill-horn has sounded for them on the other side.

Rodgers was thinking long about childhood.

I

His friend and associate, Louis MacNeice – the man who brought him to the BBC – was thinking long about his work in radio:

> The hours I have spent
> Nagged by those two black telephones on my desk
> And signing my own name in dumb consent
>
> To something or other or nothing seem burlesque
> Beside the hours they could have been, the hours
> Greek, Gothic, Roman, Norman, Romanesque . . .

On 9 October, MacNeice lunched with T.S. Eliot. They discussed the publication date of *Autumn Sequel*. At the BBC, it was a time of 'alarm and redundancy'. Gilliam was being challenged by the Drama Department, and radio was under pressure from television, which had spread rapidly after the coronation of Elizabeth II in June 1953. In the *BBC Quarterly*, MacNeice made 'A Plea for Sound':

> Sound can do many fine things which will never be possible on television. We should all therefore hope both that television may develop to the utmost and that sound broadcasting may survive.

He valued the 'goodness of the words-as-spoken-and-heard' which radio had reasserted, and emphasised the suitability of radio to 'any work . . . whose significance mainly lies in the colour and rhythm and suggestive aura of the words'.

He knew that Dylan Thomas was writing *Under Milk Wood*. When he finished it, Thomas left for America. He died in New York on 9 November 1953.

On 20 November, the Features Department in Belfast broadcast a repeat of *Return to Northern Ireland*. This had been written by Rodgers in 1950, and transmitted on the Third Programme. It was produced by Sam Hanna Bell.

The relationship was personal as well as professional. Bell and Rodgers were related by blood through their mothers. But this connection was a closely guarded secret – it might have been exploited by their bureaucratic critics.

Bell was the same age as Rodgers. He had joined the BBC after the war. He had a formidable reputation, both as producer and writer. He listened to Rodgers's talk, and suggested a new script on the theme of return. How would the poet like to return to Belfast himself – to write about his early years in Belfast?

Rodgers was immediately enthusiastic. The script would be therapy as well as good radio. The working title was *Return to Me*.

Rodgers was genuinely inventive and able. He could also be exasperating and helpless. Bell was outspoken and vigorous. He could also be supportive and resourceful. Each had what the other needed. *Return to Me* would be a joint endeavour.

Early in 1954 Rodgers was in Belfast. He met Bell, and *Return to Me* was mentioned, but Rodgers did not pursue the idea: 'I was incubating it and it hadn't yet chipped the shell.' It hatched in Essex at the end of March. He was able to send Bell detailed proposals which were close to the script as he finally wrote it:

> The programme, as I envisage it, will be in verse and prose (at least an hour in length). It will be about me, but an imaginary me, and personal details will be used only to detonate the impersonal picture; so that in the end 'I' am anybody and everybody in Belfast, and fact is fancy, and fancy fact. (Let us, for the time being, call it *The Fancy Man*.) . . . I want to run a Biblical thread through the whole thing.

Bell needed resources from the BBC Management. The Belfast Head of Programmes, Henry McMullan, was a cautious man, uneasy with big, expensive productions. He was also wary of Rodgers. Bell found it necessary to reassure him.

Rodgers was in touch with Bell again on 10 April:

> Since this is basically a personal programme and one that is slow to disclose or declare itself, I'm interested in finding a technique that will enable me to talk impersonally or even talk at all, a technique which would enable me to find out what is my mind. I can only do this by giving as loose a rein as possible to associations; in short, by using imagination as one uses it in verse.

So funding was provided for a sixty-minute script. The working title was *Return to Belfast*, and the deadline for delivery was 1 November 1954. A transmission was scheduled for early December, on the Northern Ireland Home Service only.

Rodgers opened a notebook on the programme; but nothing further happened until autumn.

In September, there were great rejoicings in London. MacNeice's *Prisoner's Progress* won the Radiotelevisione Italiana Prize and *Under Milk Wood* won the Italia Prize. Rodgers listened avidly to Thomas's programme, and it helped him to find his way with his own.

On 11 October, he had a message from Bell:

> As there is always a heavy demand for recording facilities at this time of the year, perhaps you would be good enough to let me know what discs or tapes I should have ready for you. I look forward very much to seeing you when you come to Belfast.

The wording was designed to create a mild panic. It probably succeeded, for Rodgers was moving house (he migrated to Purkiss Farmhouse, Borley, Sudbury). The script had not advanced beyond ideas. As Bell appreciated, this was unavoidable: for Rodgers's postponements were more than manoeuvres – they were necessary conditions of his existence. His work was ripened by procrastination. Bell's task was to close the lines of escape.

The theme of return had been taken up by MacNeice. On 15 October, *Return to a School* was broadcast. For this, MacNeice went back to Marlborough, and thought aloud about his boyhood there.

In Belfast, Rodgers's deadline was shifted to the middle of November. At the same time, the pressure on him increased. A rumour of his script was spread in London. It was picked up by Andrew Stewart, the Controller of the (national) Home Service. Stewart had been Controller in Belfast. He knew both Bell and Rodgers and admired their work. He made it known that he would like the tape for 'Basic', to broadcast to the whole United Kingdom.

In Belfast, the transmission was scheduled for Christmas. On 4 November, Bell wrote to Rodgers:

> Your *Return to Belfast* has been put in for week 51 . . . Could you ever drop me a note and tell me how it is progressing?

Ten days later, Rodgers wrote from Borley:

> I have numerous notes made for the Belfast programme but I do want

you to get it postponed for a short time, as I can't see it being ready for Week 51. There are many things I want to put in the programme but the things that are most evocative for me, the important trifles, are the hardest to recover. They come to mind only obliquely and timidly; and if I do try to recall them directly they shy away, leaving areas of emotional blankness where I expected to find memories.

Bell had to cope with the management. He tried to protect Rodgers, himself, and the project. On 17 December, he tackled Rodgers again:

Your feature programme has again been given a placing – this time about January 20th. Do you think there is any possibility of me having your script by that date, or failing that, could you please give me a definite date when it will be ready?

By the end of December, Rodgers was desperate:

Could you, do you think, 'dis-place' the 20th January date for the programme? I'm so sorry for the bother I'm giving you, but I'm distractingly pinched for time. ... I'm wondering if it would be possible for the programme to be scheduled for the beginning of next quarter.

In fact, the Summer Quarter was a poor location for a programme of high cost and importance. But Bell was anxious to sustain the tension. He began to press Rodgers to come over to Belfast. He stressed the importance of 'pre-production recordings'. The point was, that to make recordings possible, a 'draft script' or 'outline' would have to be written.

The plan worked, and Rodgers was forced to his desk. He completed a broad 'treatment' with dialogue. He left Borley on 27 February, travelling by train and boat. He spent a week in Belfast working with Bell, and was left in no doubt as to what was required of him. At the same time, there were many happy reunions. After one of these – a late-night session – the only copy of the script disappeared. It turned up on a windowsill in Linenhall Street, and was brought to the BBC by a bus conductor.

By April, some progress was made with the writing, and Bell was busy with the sound effects. Rodgers talked about *musique concrète*, and Bell was kicking tin cans over cobbles.

The painter Gerard Dillon was living in London. Early in June, he spent a weekend at Purkiss Farmhouse in Borley. He talked and sang, and Rodgers was entranced:

> He's the epitome of Belfast and very amusing and pleasant … He has the most Belfast voice and accent I've heard for a long time, and it plants itself immediately … In fact, as I wrote the script, I found it helpful to have Gerard Dillon's voice in my mind.

The pace of Rodgers's output began to increase. On 17 June, he wrote to Bell: 'I'm just in the throes of it, assembling the points of it, selecting, searching for shape, etc.' At last, he had a satisfactory title:

> I'm thinking of calling it *The Return Room*. 'The Return Room' in our house was an upstairs room at the end of a passage, a cul-de-sac room, in fact; it was never used by the family, but always kept for the visitors; it had a kind of foreignness about it.

He abandoned *musique concrète* and turned to homelier airs:

> Somebody pinched my *Orange Song Book* – the music one we used in *Return to Northern Ireland*. Could you ever get me one to replace it?

On 30 June, he reported again:

> For the purpose of shape I've had to invent one or two characters, including my mother. So it'll seem on the face of it, an autobiographical view of Belfast, a youthful view … There'll be a lot of snatches of singing – Gospel hymns, come-all-ye's , etc. – but they will simply blow in and out of the script like dandelion fluff, without comment, the root pattern having been established early … I want particularly in this script to use the effect of repetition, repetitions of characters and phrases and sounds. At least it's an interesting thing to try and should help to give the script a simpler line.

Bell went on leave. On 20 July, Rodgers wrote to him:

> The Belfast script's going on nicely and I aim to have it finished, and a certain amount of polishing done to it, next week.

In fact, the writing took another month. The script was completed in the third week of August. Rodgers was elated and relieved. He read it aloud for timings, and liked it. He posted it to Belfast on the 23 July:

> Dear Sam … I'm enclosing the Belfast script … In order to keep the flow of the script and to make the line of it as simple as possible I invented a few repetitive characters – Mother, Father, Ezekiel Knight, Mrs Bittercup. Since these characters are composite inventions I think it would be wise to make it clear in the announcement that the script is not a simple autobiographical return-journey. About the songs – I wonder would you try using Gerry Dillon, the painter, for the singing of them …

The script reached Bell as he was leaving Belfast, heading for Edinburgh and London. He read it at once and his response was unstinted: 'I think it is tremendous. I like every inch and line of it.'

He hurried to the Belfast docks, intending to see Rodgers at the end of the week and convey his enthusiasm in person. In Scotland, however, he heard that his wife had been admitted to hospital. He went home. Rodgers was left in the dark, and began to lose confidence in his judgement. He wrote to Bell again on 5 September:

> By concentrating on a few characters I tried to give the script a sort of rhythm and simple homogeneity. In the same way I feel that the linking effects could be simplified and I'm not at all sure whether music wouldn't have been a better choice …

On the same day, Bell wrote to him specially, describing his delight and explaining his silence.

Bell was preoccupied for some weeks. On 11 October, Rodgers wrote to him:

> If you agree, I should like to be Narrator in the programme: it's a tricky part on which all the run of the script depends, and every shade and twist of the words matters, as you know.

Bell replied two days later:

> It had never occurred to me that anyone but you should narrate *The Return Room* – it would be no show without Punch!

On 14 October, Bell recorded hymns for the programme at Gardenmore Presbyterian Church.

At Broadcasting House, the management was anxious to make the most of a prospective success. The programme was scheduled for Christmas week, for Friday, 23 December.

In London, Gerard Dillon was glad to be part of it: 'I read the script and was enchanted by it.' He suggested that his singing should be accompanied, on the guitar, by his fellow-painter, George Campbell, who was staying with him. They were recorded in London on 3 November. The English production secretary was bemused by the Ulster idiom: she logged one song as 'Fan a willow' and another as 'Daisy no a doffer'.

Dillon was so impressed that he was inspired as a draughtsman. On 9 November, he gave Rodgers a drawing which he thought might be used in the *Radio Times*. 'It's rather good,' said Rodgers, and sent it to Belfast.

On 17 November, Rodgers wrote to Bell with directions for casting:

(a) the *Mother* is important and must be a fairly flexible actress: she will have to bend into me a lot, while at the same time keeping her Scotch angularity intact.

(b) *Father* is a more rounded character and should be able to read Scripture in a rounded, impressive and sympathetic way; even though he has at times the halting difficulty of an old country-man in reading.

(c) Uncle Jacob is envisaged as a rough-and-ready hearty Ulster farmer, a cut-and-come-again character …

On 22 November, Bell wrote a 'billing' – a short description of the broadcast for *Radio Times*. He delivered an elegant formula which took care of Rodgers's worry that the programme might be regarded as personal history:

THE RETURN ROOM
A back-window on Belfast,
opened after forty years by

W.R. RODGERS
This word's-eye view of Belfast
is partly autobiographical, is
largely imaginary, and wholly true.

On 24 November, Bell relayed an appeal from his secretary:

> Miss Miller reminds me that the booking for Christmas week will probably be very heavy and suggests that you make travel arrangements early.

A week later, Bell was assembling the cast. There were contracts for Ann Maguire, Bill Hunter, James Mageean, Elizabeth Begley, Kitty Gibson, James Boyce, J.G. Devlin, James McCrudden, Bill McKay Kenny, and Charles Witherspoon.

On 2 December, there was a frantic telegram from Rodgers: 'MAY I FLY ACROSS 19TH? STEAMER BERTHS UNAVAILABLE.' The BBC, of course, was obliged to say yes, and sent him an insurance form 'against flying'.

The programme was acquiring significance. In addition to the interest shown by Andrew Stewart, it attracted the attention of the Overseas Service. Potentially, the audience became worldwide.

On Wednesday, 7 September, Bell auditioned child actors. Three were selected – Billy McGuigan (aged 14), Marilyn Smyth (10½), and Denis Maguire (10).

On 14 December, at 5.30 p.m., twenty-four children arrived at Broadcasting House. They were from two Belfast schools, Harding Memorial on the Cregagh Road, and St Comgall's in Divis Street. They rehearsed skipping songs, rhymes, and chants. For the sake of authenticity, they worked in 'the yard'. They were accompanied by half a dozen members of the Ulster Singers, who rehearsed hymns.

The children, and the Ulster Singers, were recorded on 15 December, between 7 p.m. and 10 p.m. They were joined by a trumpeter, Hugh McAuley.

Bell was at his desk on Sunday. The following day – 19 December – Rodgers arrived.

The use of tape was in its infancy, and the full possibilities had not been developed. Twenty years later, *The Return Room* would have been recorded in short sections. In 1955, however, the practice was to pre-record brief 'inserts', then rehearse the whole production exhaustively. It was finally recorded from a live transmission.

The rehearsals took four days – over twenty hours in studio. The first session was on 20 December, from 6 p.m to 10.30 p.m. The second was on 21 December, from 2 p.m. to 10.30 p.m. (when the cast was joined by a drummer, Patrick O'Kane). The third was on 22 December, from 6 p.m. to 10.30 p.m. To the satisfaction of all concerned, it was confirmed that the tape was wanted by the Overseas Service. A large proportion of the extra fees was spent in celebration at the BBC Club.

On Friday, 23 December, rehearsals were from 6 p.m. to 9 p.m. Thereafter tension mounted rapidly. The red lights went on over the studio doors. At 9.15, the show was on the air.

> What was in print
> Must take on breath and what was thought be said.
> In the end there was the Word, at first a glint,
>
> Then an illumination overhead
> Where the high towers are lit …

In London, Louis MacNeice was editing galaxies – a Christmas programme called *The Star We Follow*. He used recordings made at Jodrell Bank, with echoes from the edge of outer space – an ultimate return, to the start of the universe.

> They are gone, the old residenters. The mill-horn has sounded for them on the other side. But I would give a sugar-bag of polite talk for just one nip of their bitter old puritan tongues, one pull of their racy old pipes.

For Rodgers, the 'old residenters' were the giants of his boyhood. For broadcasters of a later generation, they are Bertie himself, Sam Bell, Louis MacNeice, and the actors who thronged *The Return Room*. For these too, the mill-horn has sounded. But at least we can savour the nip of their tongues – one pull of their racy old pipes.

This introduction is an extended version of the essay previously published as 'The Pursuit of The Fancy Man' in *The Honest Ulsterman*, No. 92 (1991).

I am indebted to Fergus and Angélique Hanna Bell, and to BBC Northern Ireland. Other sources include the Calendar of Wills in the Public Record Office of Northern Ireland; the newspaper files in the Linen Hall Library; Barbara Coulton's *Louis MacNeice in the BBC* (Faber, 1980); Rex Cathcart's *The Most Contrary Region* (Blackstaff, 1984); and records of conversations with Sam Hanna Bell.

A family portrait with W.R. Rodgers in the pram with his older sister, Elsbeth;
above, his twin sister Reah

BIOGRAPHICAL
NOTE

W.R. Rodgers was born on 1 August 1909 in the Mountpottinger
area of east Belfast. His parents, both of whom were from farming
backgrounds, were strict Presbyterians. Robert Skelly Rodgers, from
the townland of Artana, near Dromara, in County Down, was a
childless widower when in 1906 he married Jane McCarey from
the Dundonald area of County Down. They had four children,
Elsbeth (who died aged seven), twins Rachel (Reah) and William
Robert, always known as Bertie, and Jean.

Rodgers was educated at Mountpottinger public elementary school
and Queen's University. His father wanted him to follow in his
footsteps and make a career in insurance but his mother was eager
that he should become a Presbyterian minister. It was on the
understanding that Rodgers would go into the church that they were
prepared to make the financial sacrifices entailed in sending him to
Queen's.

W.R. Rodgers at Mountpottinger public elementary school,
second row from top, third from the left

In 1931 Rodgers graduated with a BA in English literature. By the
time he began his theological training at Assembly's College in Belfast
he had already been drawn into a tightly knit student group involved
with the dramatic society and into the editing of a university
magazine. Mildly left-wing and sexually emancipated, the group
included his future wife, medical student Marie Waddell.

Even before becoming an assistant minister in Lurgan in County
Armagh (1934) and then acquiring his own church in nearby
Loughgall (1935), Rodgers was leading something of a double life,
one part of him drawn to the Presbyterian ministry, the other to a
more secular world. *The Return Room*, in which the narrator declares
'a fellow might go and get himself into jail just to escape from so
much goodness', suggests that Rodgers's hankering after such
adventuring could be traced to his early childhood. However,
Rodgers was in many ways suited to his calling and the apple country
of Armagh fostered his love of nature. He warmed to his congregation,
enjoying, as well as distrusting, his status as a minister. In the spacious
Georgian manse at Cloveneden church Rodgers entertained his
Belfast friends. At weekends they would arrive, discussing socialist
theory, anti-fascist politics, Freudian psychology and the future of
Spanish Republican refugees whom some of them had received into
their own homes. But, on Sunday morning, when Rodgers

W.R. Rodgers's installation as minister of Cloveneden Presbyterian Church,
Loughgall, County Armagh, 1935

disappeared down the lane to preach the faith of his fathers in the
eighteenth-century church with its box pews, his visitors were strictly
forbidden to attend.

County Armagh also provided Rodgers with important literary
contacts – the artists Mercy and George McCann lived nearby at
Vinnycash and introduced him to their friend Louis MacNeice – and
his exchanges with them stimulated his interest in writing. His wife
Marie, whom he had married in 1935, moved into the manse with a
sheaf of short stories, prompting Rodgers to try his hand at the form.
But neither he nor Marie managed to get their stories published.
Then Rodgers turned to poetry and it quickly brought him acclaim.
His first published poem 'The Far-off Hills' – a denunciation of
violence, dictatorship and hypocrisy that would help to define him as
a war poet – appeared in *The Listener* in 1938. Some months later
John Hewitt, listening to a Radio Éireann poetry programme made
up of prize-winning entries to a competition, recognised 'An Irish
Lake', submitted by one William Rodgers, as the work of his friend
Bertie.

In 1938 Rodgers and Marie had a daughter, Harden. Nini followed
in 1940. Rodgers's first collection of poems, *Awake! And other Poems*
(Secker and Warburg), appeared in 1941, delayed by a year because

the first printing had been destroyed in the blitz of Portsmouth in 1940. In 1941 Rodgers also visited Dublin for the first time, staying with Geoffery Taylor, poetry editor of the *Bell*, for some weeks, an experience which he repeated in 1942. These visits marked the beginning of Rodgers's involvement in the world of Irish Letters, a contribution that was formally recognised when he was elected to the Irish Academy of Letters in 1953 and awarded an annual stipend from the Dublin Arts Council in 1968.

In 1943 Rodgers left Northern Ireland again, setting off for England for the first time. He had been granted prolonged leave of absence from his congregation to take Marie, who had become ill, to Oxford for treatment. While in England Rodgers visited the office of the *New Statesman,* which had already taken an interest in his poetry, and the editor suggested he should write a prose piece on Northern Ireland. The result was the 1944 essay 'Black North', which described the division between the two communities in Northern Ireland and criticised the Unionist government for living off, rather than trying to decrease, sectarianism. It was only when he returned home to Loughgall that he realised how bitterly this article had offended his congregation.

In 1945 his first BBC script, featuring Armagh, *The City set on the Hill,* was produced in Belfast by Louis MacNeice, who was then

Louis MacNeice with W.R. Rodgers in a BBC studio

involved in the BBC's *Third Programme* in London. Through MacNeice's good offices, Lawrence Gilliam, Head of Features, offered Rodgers a position as a producer and scriptwriter. After some months of hesitation Rodgers decided to accept and left Loughgall permanently. Based in London, he worked for the BBC from 1946 until 1952, the year in which he published his second and final collection of poems, *Europa and the Bull and Other Poems* (Secker & Warburg).

Trained by MacNeice and Gilliam, Rodgers became a skilled broadcaster and scriptwriter. He made programmes in Britain and on the continent. For his spring programme in 1948 he travelled from Lapland to Italy recording the changing seasons, and composed a sequence of fourteen poems entitled *Resurrection, an Easter Sequence*. But it was in Ireland that he developed what came to be known as the 'Rodgers technique', paring back the role of narrator to allow the voices of the interviewees to flood the programme, as in his Belfast-produced *Hired and Bound*, which caught the memories of those who had gone to the hiring fairs. In his innovative and critically acclaimed *Irish Literary Portraits* he perfected this technique, juxtaposing voices that gave conflicting views of a great writer in an attempt to create a more complex portrait. Rodgers also used this device to give the impression of people in intimate conversation when in fact they were miles apart or possibly not on speaking terms with one another.

In January 1953 Rodgers and his wife Marie were divorced, after a long period of estrangement. For some time Rodgers had been having an affair with Lawrence Gilliam's wife, Marianne. When she left her husband for Rodgers, Louis MacNeice advised Bertie to resign from the BBC, which he did, and for over a decade he lived as a freelance writer and broadcaster. After his divorce, Rodgers and Marianne married and in 1954 they moved to Suffolk and in 1959 to Essex. Their daughter Lucy was born in 1956. These were difficult years for Rodgers, fraught with the financial insecurity of a freelance life. But they were also the years in which Rodgers produced some of his finest radio work, including some of his *Irish Literary Portraits*, which ran from 1949 to 1966 and which were published posthumously in 1972, and *The Return Room* which was first broadcast in 1955.

W.R. Rodgers at Pitzer College, California, 1966

In 1966 Rodgers found a solution to his financial difficulties when he was appointed writer in residence at Pitzer College, Claremont, California, arriving during the era of the Summer of Love and the Vietnam protests. By 1968, as he listened to the news of rising trouble in Northern Ireland, he knew that he was ill with cancer. Rodgers died in California on 1 February 1969 and is buried in Loughgall.

Marianne Rodgers, W.R. Rodgers, Erna Naughton and Gerard Dillon
at Purkiss Farmhouse, Essex, 1955

THE
RETURN ROOM

PRODUCED BY SAM HANNA BELL

TRANSMISSION: FRIDAY 23 DECEMBER, 1955, 9.15–10.15 p.m.

W.R. Rodgers in the BBC studio

ANNOUNCER

The BBC presents *The Return Room*, a programme in which
W.R. Rodgers opens a back-window on Belfast.

My Lagan Love

sung by Gerard Dillon

Where Lagan stream sings lullaby
There dwells a lily fair
The dew of eve is in her eye
The night is on her hair
And like a love-sick lennan-shee
She has my heart in thrall
No life I own nor liberty
For love is lord of all.

Light anvil beat

NARRATOR

Once upon a time when catch was can, and rabbits ran, and a
farthing was a fortune, I was born – to the tinkling symbol of a
blacksmith's forge in Belfast.

MOTHER

I wonder was I right
Having him at all,
I was brought up tight
And I kept myself small –

NARRATOR

Thomas John Todd, they called me; son to Adam Todd.

BELFAST CHILD (girl)

Holy Mary, Mother of God,
Pray for me and Tommy Todd:
Tommy Todd is a Prod,
Holy Mary, Mother of God.

NARRATOR

There was a halo of hills round me from the start, and a hug-me-tight of holiness. All the pubs held their breath that day, and the bells of the city danced with their hands in their pockets, and the soothering river ran wild, and a decorated tramcar took off over the hills and far away. My father – who had a fine sense of occasion –

FATHER

We may put a nick in the post today!

NARRATOR

– My father got down the Good Book and read from the roll of the generations of great men.

Muster roll of drums to voice reading

FATHER

… Juda, which was the son of Jacob, which was the son of Isaac, which was the son of Abraham, which was the son of Thara, which was the son of Nachor which was the son of Garuch … which was the son of Methusala which was the son of Enoch which was the son of Jared which was the son of Enos which was the son of Seth which was the son of Adam which was the son of God.

NARRATOR

Son of Adam; Sin of Adam,
I was the heir to all that Adamnation
And hand-me-down of doom; the old newcomer
To the return room.
The apple blushed for me below Bellevue;
Grey Lagan was my Jordan, Connswater
My washpot, and over Castlereagh
I cast out my shoe.

Drums behind

Humdrummery of history:
Three hundred years ago my foundling fathers,
With farthing fists, and thistles in their eyes,
Were wished upon this foreshore;
Bibles for bibs and bloody pikes for rattles,
And tombs for keeps. There was not time
To wade through wedding to a birth:
The God of battles took the banns for read,
Calvin and culverin sang the cradle song
And Cromwell made the bed:
Put to a frugal breast of swollen hopes
They did their levelling best.

And I, Thomas John Todd,
Made in the image of God ...

BELFAST WOMAN

Och, that toty wee thing! The spit an' image of his da!

NARRATOR

... Was tied to the tail of the blue and orange cart
Of history, articled to etiquette;
One part of me, the innumerable boy,
Tethered to a Christian name and hope,
While all the lucky ones went dancing off
Scot-free behind the bushes –

MOTHER

I wonder was I right
Having him at all,
I was brought up tight
And I kept myself small.

I never had ache
Or pain that I know
Till I heard the corncrake
In the field below.

Corncrake, craking

NARRATOR

In the dead of summer the midnight fields round Belfast creaked
and rocked like a rusty bedspring with that intolerable sound. Ache,
ache – the waking guilt at the back of the Puritan urge, the nagging
voice that drove the restless generations from up-country into the
gospel-singing city on the river. There is always forgiveness,
downriver.

Salvation Army hymn, 'Shall we gather at the river?'
(sung by The Ulster Singers)

On the margin of the river,
Washing up its silver spray,
We will walk and worship ever,
All the happy golden day.

Yes, we'll gather at the river,
The beautiful, the beautiful river;
Gather with the saints at the river
That flows by the throne of God.

Tugboats whooping

NARRATOR

Our house stood on a sandy ridge overlooking the river valley.
High up in the back gable, at the end of the corridor, there was the
'Return Room'. It led nowhere but back again; a dead-end room,

kept for visitors. But from the window I could see across the city. Goat's tow of a city that leaped from gutter to gantry at one go. City with the brick-red face and the bowler hat of smoke. City of ships and shawlies, doles and doyleys –

BELFAST MAN

Ah sure, isn't it all a jar o' worms anyway . . .

NARRATOR

From the back-street far below me came the grasshopper chirp of the blacksmith's anvil. I could see Mary Marley, the ragwoman, pushing her handcart of crockery.

MARY MARLEY

New delph! New delph! Any ould rags? New delph!

NARRATOR

Behind her walked the black man with his brush –

SWEEP

Sweep! Sweep! Sweep!

Empty tin can kicked across the cobbles

NARRATOR

And shining like a shilling in a sweep's hand the empty tin went clattering across the cobblestones, scandalising my mother.

Tin kicked again

MOTHER

I'll warrant you it's that hooligan Mickey Clark. If he's not cloddin' things, he's kickin' them. It's a wonder his people wouldn't think

shame, and him scouring the streets from dawn till dark. Never in the house for a minute.

NARRATOR

'Ha,' says my father softly —

FATHER

If that's his only sin —

MOTHER

An only sin is like an only child, Adam. It's apt to be indulged.

FATHER

Give him time and he'll soon get a wheen more to keep it company. Woman dear, the way you go on about things!

NARRATOR

My country mother was always on the go, like a bird. She was a wonder for goodness and would have given you the bite out of her mouth. But it was a sad little Presbyterian mouth. Even when she smiled it was as if the 'weaks' of her mouth were sore with apprehension of the things that might happen to a body in this world of sin and sorrow. Every evening, when my father sat down to read the *Belfast Telegraph* my mother would say to him —

MOTHER

Can I have the deaths, Adam?

NARRATOR

And my father would hand over the middle page with the obituaries in it. It was her way of keeping in touch with life.

MOTHER

Ochanee! Do you see this, Adam? – 'Suddenly, at his residence, the Whins, Moneydig, Moses Andrew McWhirter'.

FATHER

Woman dear, you don't say! And him walkin' the markets no more'n a week ago. And doing so well, too.

MOTHER

He was doin' too well. Every penny was a prisoner. And him with neither chick nor child to feed.

FATHER

Aye, a close man, Mosey. I knowed him put the light out afore sayin' his prayers at night, just to save the oil. Ah well, it doesn't do to be talkin'.

NARRATOR

'So poor Mosey's gone,' says my father.

FATHER

He was a good neighbour. I mind well when his grand-da and mine fell out, the one would miscall the other for a Croppy Boy. And that takes you back a bit.

NARRATOR

And lying in bed that night, I would hear my father reading to himself from the Book – he could only read aloud – and his voice rising and falling, mingled with the moan of the wind in the gable.

Sound of wind, rising intermittently

FATHER

… As for man, his days are as grass: as a flower of the field, so he flourisheth. For the wind passeth over it and it is gone, and the place thereof shall know it no more. But the mercy of the Lord is from everlasting to everlasting upon them that fear him, and his righteousness unto children's children.

Shipyard horn, prolonged

NARRATOR

That was the resurrection-sound which wakened me each morning – the Island horn. And in the dark of a winter's morning I could hear the tramp of hundreds of feet going past to their lives in the shipyard.

Mrs Mulligan, a mile away, crossed herself uneasily as the Protestant feet tramped past her house. And her twelve children fell quiet under the bedclothes, for fear the feet might quicken and break into a run.

Nothing was humdrum in those long away and far ago days. The morning rose up early for me, and the world went out of its way to call me. I could hardly wait to finish my porridge. Not that I liked porridge –

MOTHER

You can either like it or lump it. There's many a wee bare-foot fella would be glad of it.

NARRATOR

The wee bare-footed fellows lived in the low-down streets at the back of our house. But our front road was a high-up and respectable one. All the boys in it wore boots. I could hear them now, running after Barney Hassan's breadcart – a long kite-tail of mockery.

Crack of horsewhip

GIRLS (children from St Comgall's)
Barney Hassan's bread
Sticks to the belly like lead
Not a bit of wonder
That you belch like thunder
When you eat Barney Hassan's bread.

NARRATOR
Crack would go the whip about their scattering legs. Once upon a time the vanishing cream of high society had lived in these high houses, and the relics of old decency still lingered on the tongue of Mrs Bittercup.

MRS BITTERCUP
I declare to God you would wonder what the place is coming to, Mrs Todd. It's getting so common, nowadays, what with lodgers and policemen and the like. Would you look at yon one, now!

NARRATOR
Maisie Modesty with her bubble baby had emerged to take the air.

MRS BITTERCUP
The impertinence! Manifestin' herself and her with never a marriage-line to her name.

MOTHER
There's talk of her getting married.

MRS BITTERCUP
Marry! And who would marry that come-all-ye, even if her hide was made of gold and twelve men diggin' at it.

NARRATOR

In the distance two nuns, in dark waving habits, appeared.

MRS BITTERCUP

Wouldn't they give you the creeps, Mrs Todd? Like big black billows of feminine death. Well! If it isn't that brat Mickey Clark! Tryin' to squeeze past between them, just for devilment. Can you beat it!

MOTHER

Is there no manners or courtesy left in the country at all?

MRS BITTERCUP

What's he up to now?

NARRATOR

Mickey was following now on the heels of little Mr Jellybelly who was pretending not to hear a word he said:

MICKEY

I wonder would you rather
Or rather would you be
Legs up to your oxter
Or belly to your knee.

MRS BITTERCUP

God help the wee man! Sure if he was any smaller you'd have to cut the grass to see him. Well, it wouldn't do if we was all the same.

NARRATOR

Nothing was ever the same in Belfast, for the place had character. The very stones in the street exerted themselves and rose up in cobbles – 'pavers' we called them – and the great roads grumbled along on granite setts. Many's a time my knees would be dangling

with blood-and-iodine ribbons, for I was born very close to the ground and I knew the flagstones like the palm of my hand. You had to know what crack in the pavement not to walk on, for this one was lucky and that one unlucky; this stone was good for spinning tops and that one for skipping games.

GIRLS (children from Harding Memorial)
I know a woman with a big red nose,
Lookin' for a house in Sandy Row,
A house to let, apply within,
A woman put out for drinkin' gin,
Apply to Tommy Todd within.

NARRATOR
And in I would jump, into the skipping rope. In those days four flagstones from the garden gate was foreign ground, and the other side of the street was a new-found-land. At the bottom of the hill the world went by. Three main roads met here, and three corner pubs supplied the bottle-neck for the belly of traffic. There was a cab-rank for jaunting cars and the skinny three-cornered horses stood sleeping with one limp leg all day long, while the jarveys collogued in the pubs.

1ST JARVEY
You're wrong, now, if you ask me.

2ND JARVEY
Have a titter of wit. I'm not askin', I'm tellin' ye. A white horse is ever and always kept for weddings and Sundays.

NARRATOR
Horses of the sun. And round the corner would come ancient history in the shape of the May Queen, dressed in white, with her singing horde of ragamuffins in attendance.

RAGAMUFFINS (children from Harding Memorial)
If you want to see King William
Take a tram down to the Junction,
There you'll see a noble soldier
Riding on a big white horse.

Rattle of money-box

BOY
Give us a penny, mister! Give us a penny!

Rattle again, to the tinkle of an anvil

NARRATOR
That was the thing about Belfast: in spite of the trams and the motors it was a city of horses, and the tinkling symbol was the blacksmith's forge.

In the half-darkness of the morning I could hear them going down to the docks and the markets; Clydesdales, donkeys, spring vans, springless carts, pantechnicons – the whole hoof-roar of a city getting on its feet.

Noise of horse traffic

An odd day I might happen on a crowd gathered round a fallen horse. I would watch the great beast sprachling to get to its feet with the sparks flying from under him like a blaze of fleas.

CARTER
Take a hoult of his head or he'll hurt himself. Keep him down, keep him down, man, till I get the collar off him.

BYSTANDER
What happened?

CARTER

Ah sure the ould horse has no debate with his legs. How could he, on them greasy setts?

NARRATOR

In the afternoon a solitary horse-woman from the riding stables would canter past like Dignity. That was the moment Mickey Clark was waiting for. He knew the horse, for it had once been the milkman's horse.

MICKEY

Pint please!

NARRATOR

And the horse would stop dead on its rockers. You see, the afternoons in Belfast seemed to hang on our hands. It was as if the day had lost the memory of its end and errand. But the evening had its bright and sudden excitements. Maybe big Uncle Jacob from the country would breeze in to see us.

JACOB

How are you Adam and how's all here?

FATHER

Come on in, Jacob, and set yourself down, man.

MOTHER

But you may just take us as you find us.

NARRATOR

Jacob had a big red cup of a nose that wasn't, said my mother, due to drinking water. And his great fingers fascinated me. They had warts on the back of them, like bracken, as if there was ferny blood in the man. Come easy, go easy. Care was his thirty-second cousin.

FATHER

You're keeping bravely, Jacob?

JACOB

Ach, the ould legs aren't as loyal as they were, Adam. A scringe of gout in the big toe, betimes. But sure there's none of us gettin' any younger.

MOTHER

Or any wiser, Jacob. A bit less sugar in the tea would do wonders.

NARRATOR

After tea I took him out to show him the sights. Old Mrs Ruth's house. Nobody knew her. She had come here from the country thirty years ago and never once put her nose outside the door since. Belfast was alien ground to her. Did Jacob know her? Aye, he did. And what was she like?

JACOB

She sits wi' her toes in the ashes
And her hands tucked under her chin,
And if anyone asks what ails her,
She rifts — and says, 'it's the wind'.

NARRATOR

But the finest sight of all I kept to the last — the house where Maisie lived who had the baby and wasn't married. Jacob was laughing when we came home.

MOTHER

Was he showin' you that woman's house, Jacob?

JACOB

He was in sowl!

MOTHER

How often have I warned you, Tommy, never to –

NARRATOR

'Ah,' says my father –

FATHER

Let him be. He'll learn soon enough.

JACOB

Milk in the basin, sugar in the cup,
Never run your rabbit when the rhubarb's up!

MOTHER

For shame, Jacob! In front of the child!

NARRATOR

'And how,' says my father, trying to carry it off –

FATHER

How's the wee moyley cow doin', Jacob? She was a fine lookin'
heifer.

JACOB

She's like the women nowadays, Adam. She puts all she has on her
back. Damn the sign of a calf though she's been to the Bachelor
twice.

NARRATOR

I could have listened to Jacob till the cows came home. But that
was the one night my mother hurried me off to bed. And I lay
listening to the far-off ring of their voices, talking about the old
times, and the old residenters, and the old doings. It was late when I
fell asleep; so late that I heard little Mr Jellybelly, full of glow-worm

whiskey and nightingale ale, tumbling home in the dark, singing as if to waken the dead.

JELLYBELLY
Oft in the stilly night,
When slumbers sweet surround me,
Fond memory brings the light
Of other days around me.

Thunderous knocking on door

NARRATOR
God help us all! He had come to the wrong door.

MRS BITTERCUP
Yon was a carry-on! It beats me, Mrs Todd, how she puts up with it.

MOTHER
A body has to bleed inwardly sometimes, Mrs Bittercup.

NARRATOR
Eliza Bittercup had come out to look the morning over. She was watching Mrs Jellybelly polishing the door-knocker.

MRS BITTERCUP
It's no life for a respectable woman, Mrs Todd.

MOTHER
Och well, sure we have to have a bit of give and take in this world.

MRS BITTERCUP
I know what *I'd* give him. Not an inch! Mr Once-a-fortnight!

NARRATOR

My mother, bless her, was so respectable that if you'd been running for your life she'd have stopped you to tell you your bootlaces weren't tied.

MOTHER

What'll the neighbours think! Tie them up at once Tommy. And what's that fell out of your pocket? Well, for cryin' out loud! If it isn't a cigarette. How dare you, at your age! You're a caution!

NARRATOR

I found it, says I.

MOTHER

I wonder what the minister would say if he knew.

NARRATOR

Anyway, says I, the minister smokes. Mickey Clark says –

MOTHER

What! Is it that blather-me-skite that's talking? Goin' about with a pin on a stick pickin' up fag-ends from the gutter. I'll give him a cooler if I catch him.

NARRATOR

In the little street a mile away Mrs Mulligan would be talking to *her* twelve children.

MRS MULLIGAN

I can't turn my back for a minute but you're up to some badness. Which one of you took the sixpence I put on the mantelpiece? Own up, now, at once. Was it you, Mary? You Malachy? Aloysius? Bridget? Maureen? – Isn't there one of you with a tongue in your head? Get down there, the lot of you, on your knees.

45

NARRATOR

And down on their knees they went in front of the holy image, while Mrs Mulligan offered up a prayer.

MRS MULLIGAN

O sufferin' Saviour, you who had twelve of your own and one of them let you down, in your infinite mercy point out to me now which one of these children took the sixpence –

MAUREEN

I tuk it, Ma!

NARRATOR

In those simple unpsychological days your parents never followed you around leaving you alone. No. Belfast mothers knew what was good for you, and they gave you the compulsory choice of heaven. We learned our catechism early.

MOTHER

'What is the chief end of man?'

TOMMY

'Man's chief end is to glorify God and to enjoy him forever.'

MOTHER

Adam! Will you see who's at the door?

NARRATOR

It was Ezekiel Knight, the local undertaker. My father was in the life insurance business, so it was only natural that the two of them should be on good terms. Mr Knight was an imposing man. He had a double bib of chins; and an expensive gold watchchain flashed on the expansive pan of his belly. His laughter was likened to the gleam of moonlight on a tombstone. Father and he always had their little joke.

FATHER

You know what the Good Book says, Mr Knight: – 'And there shall be no night there.'

KNIGHT

Aha, Mr Todd. Neither shall there be marriage or giving in marriage. – He'd always a good eye for a woman, Mrs Todd.

FATHER

And where would you or your trade be if it weren't for the women? Tell me that.

MOTHER

I see wee Jimmy McCooey's dead. You know, the one in Nettle Street.

KNIGHT

Say no more, say no more. As decent a man, Mrs Todd, as ever turned a penny.

MOTHER

Ay, they say he drank a street of houses in his time.

KNIGHT

Oh, he had his faults, no doubt. A fine big belt of a fellow once, with fists on him like flails, and knuckles like harrows. But what between drink and the police he dwindled away to nothing.

FATHER

Ay, twenty years ago he'd have been the awkward man to handle.

KNIGHT

Now I can slide him into the casket as easy as a bar of soap. Say no more, say no more.

NARRATOR

'Listen,' says my mother, reading from the *Telegraph*: 'At his parents' residence, Kinnagore, David, dearly beloved son of Jonathan and Jane Stewart … Well well.'

MOTHER

'Funeral private.' Dear me! What's the world comin' to?

KNIGHT

Funerals, Mrs Todd, aren't what they used to be. By rights, a man's demise is not a private matter. I mind when I was a young fellow there wouldn't be a hand's turn of work done in the townland on the day of a death. But there's no respect left in this city. No respect at all.

NARRATOR

All the same a funeral in our street was a State Occasion. All the respectability of the neighbourhood would be there: my father in his best dickey and black silk hat, Mr Knight in his topper and frock-coat, Mr Redmond the evergreengrocer, Mr Blue the butcher, thin Mr White —

Now ever since the day his doctor told him he should take more outings for the good of his health, thin Mr White had taken to going to funerals. Oh, I envied him all the rides he got in carriages. I looked at the lovely black horses with the frothy bibs and the silver harness and the delicate feet dancing adagios and I longed to have a great grief of my own. Above all, to sit perched up high, beside the mighty coachman, to see the long procession walking behind me, and the footpaths crowded with silent citizens who took off their hats.

Gerard Dillon

Maybe we'd meet another funeral, and the drivers would dip their whips in common grief, and continue to look sternly ahead of them, never batting an eyelid. Sceptre and crown might tumble down, but the hearse-driver never. People were dying to get these men to drive them, drive them over the hill and far away, away through the gates of day to the back and black of beyond –

MOTHER

Whatever are you dreamin' about Tommy? Run on down to the chemists at the Bridge, and get me that bottle they've made up. Here's the money. You can buy yourself a stick of liquorice. And don't be long.

NARRATOR

The road to anywhere was long in those days. There were boys playing 'piggy' or trundling hoops, or trinkling marbles along the gutter, or speelying up lampposts, or blowing cigarette cards. Everything had its place and season. The girls this day were skipping and singing as usual –

GIRLS (children of Harding Memorial)
King Billy was a gentleman
He wore a watch and chain,
The Pope he was a beggarman
And lived in Chapel Lane.

NARRATOR

And there were spinning tops, red, blue, yellow, green, with fancy patterns chalked on them, flogged along the wrinkly pavements. At the end of one faraway street I passed the Mulligan children skipping.

CHILDREN (from St Comgall's School)
Up the long ladder and down the short rope,
Away with King Billy and God bless the Pope.

NARRATOR
We had our own streets, of course, and we kept ourselves to
ourselves, sidling past each other when we met, like tiptoed terriers
bristling with indifference.

BOY
Hi, boy! Give us a lick o' your liquorice.

NARRATOR
I took no notice. It was better that way. A lick could lead to
anything.

BOY
Ya, booh! Up the long ladder and down the short rope,
Away with King Billy and God bless the Pope.

NARRATOR
A strange assistant served me in the shop. For Mr Easyman, the
chemist, was deep in talk with a customer.

CUSTOMER
I want some lead acetate, if you've got it, Mr Easyman.

EASYMAN
I suppose you're aware that's not a thing we hand out to everybody
without enquiry? You see, the inspectors are gettin' very particular.

CUSTOMER
Och, I know all about that. But tell me, how can I get some?

EASYMAN

Now now now, sure haven't you got an ould horse with a sprained shoulder?

CUSTOMER

Man dear. I've got two of them.

EASYMAN

Right you are. How much do you want?

NARRATOR

I kept thinking about those two horses, all the way home.

MOTHER

I declare to my clogs, Tommy, you're the world's worst slowcoach. You'd be a good one to send for sorrow. What kept you? Did you bring me the change?

NARRATOR

No, says I.

MOTHER

And why not? Didn't I tell you –

NARRATOR

You told me never to take money from a strange man.

MOTHER

Well, for two pins – ! Away back at once and get it.

NARRATOR

There was one thing about Belfast that puzzled me. A person might be walking calmly along the road, thinking about things, like

kali-suckers, or conkers, or comics, or whatnots, and suddenly
out of the blue would come a voice that curled him up like
a caterpillar.

VOICE
Sinner, flee from the wrath to come!

If in sin you longer wait,
You may find no open gate,
And your cry be just too late.
Be in time!

This day, this moment –

NARRATOR
The day suddenly lost its meaning and died. Brightness fell from
the air. But not for long.

RAGAMUFFINS
Our queen can birl her leg, birl her leg, birl her leg,
Our queen can birl her leg, birl her leg.

NARRATOR
Round the corner would come the springtime troop of ragamuffins
with the May Queen dancing at their head. She wore a bridal dress
of dirty old lace curtains and a wreath of paper flowers. Her
bridesmaids held up her hands and danced beside her. And her
paramour, with his face blackened, followed with a rowdy crowd of
retainers rattling money-boxes.

BOY
Give us a penny, mister.

NARRATOR

It was the one time in the year when the stranger was welcome within our gates.

RAGAMUFFINS

The darkie says he'll marry her, marry her, marry her
The darkie says he'll marry her, because she is a queen.

NARRATOR

Everything was suddenly light and gay and capering. The tram conductors put on white caps; painters appeared on the tops of ladders, like angels; and all the dogs of the neighbourhood took to crossing the road at once –

Spring had come. The air turned over a new leaf, all the walls were down, and winter's wadding off, and we ran weightless through the bare-legged streets and mooned in the warm watery shadows among the market crowds. The forge glowed in the back-street and the red cock crowed in Mrs McCurdy's backyard. Up the Resurrection and the Rose! –

VOICE

Up the rebels!

NARRATOR

– And the dancing world had hours of idleness in it.

RAGAMUFFINS

Our queen can birl her leg, birl her leg, birl her leg,
Our queen can birl her leg, birl her leg.

NARRATOR

But always, far away at the end of my morning shadow, I could see the evening figure of God walking in the cool of the day.

MOTHER

Tell him to come in at once, Adam.

NARRATOR

I wilted a bit when I was suddenly pulled into the house.
'What for?' I asked.

MOTHER

You're goin' to the gospel meeting.

NARRATOR

'But look,' I'd say desperately, 'we're just beginning a game. A game
of rounders.'

MOTHER

It'd suit you better to be thinkin' of your latter-end. Like it or lump
it you're goin'. And that's that.

NARRATOR

It was then that I felt the bitterness of the world. I knew now why
a fellow might go and get himself into jail just to escape from so
much goodness. Well, just wait till I grew up: I'd show them.
Maybe, maybe when I was dead they'd see differently. Yes, that was
it. A sudden, extravagant, but not too final death. I could see the
whole picture – the drawn blinds, my mother's sorry face, dark fires
burning in the house, and a grief of talk in upper rooms. And
Ezekiel Knight, the undertaker, would be there, and Elizabeth
Bittercup.

KNIGHT

Say no more, Mrs Todd, say no more. He was a good son to you,
was Tommy. The best.

MRS BITTERCUP

He was too good for this world. I never knowed a boy to have so much wisdom for his years, Mrs Todd.

KNIGHT

It's needed in the other world, too. But he'll be missed, he'll surely be missed, Mrs Todd.

MOTHER

What are you dreamin' about, Tommy? Standing there with one arm as long as the other! Go on and get on you or we'll be late for the meeting!

NARRATOR

Then I'd be herded down the holiday street with many a hungry look back, like a young goat looking for a gate, a gap, or a getaway. The church was quiet. A quiet so solemn and compelling that even Mrs Bittercup confided her cough to her hankie. It was as if the still centuries had been waiting for us there, all the time, like a clock in an empty schoolroom. It wasn't half bad. The world took on a faraway and overall look. It was the week before Easter, and the sound of the ritual hymn inside mingled bitterly and agreeably with the ritual song of the street children.

WORSHIPPERS (Gardenmore Presbyterian Church)
There is a green hill far away
Without a city wall,
Where our dear Lord was crucified
Who died to save us all.

RAGAMUFFINS
Our queen can birl her leg, birl her leg, birl her leg,
Our queen can birl her leg, birl her leg.

Gerard Dillon.

NARRATOR

Belfast was like that – a criss-cross place. We ignored Good Friday
as being too near to Rome, but Easter was a high day in our
calendar. Every Easter morning we would take a tram to the end of
the lines. We would walk outside the city till we reached the
Dundonald cemetery, and there we would roll our coloured eggs
down a grassy slope till they broke. What possessed my mother I
don't know, but it was something as old as the hills, and older than
the hymn itself. For if our eggs failed to break, we would take them
to a great tumulus, or prehistoric burial-ground, which topped the
distant fields, and there we would finish the job. Then after
surveying the family grave (and pocketing two white flint stones
from it to strike sparks with) I would walk back through the broken
egg-shells of light and shadow to the dusty terminus, with its litter
of old tram-tickets and its squalling crowd of youngsters.

BELFAST WOMAN

Look if yous don't behave yourselves I'll never bring yous out
again! Carryin' on like that! Give it over now, you've my head
turned ...

NARRATOR

And that night my father would get down the Book. This time it
would be the book of metrical paraphrases. He loved these, I think,
even more than the Bible itself, for there was a proper kind of
concentrated gloom about them. They made no concessions to life.

FATHER

Few are thy days and full of woe,
O man of woman born!
Thy doom is written, 'Dust thou art,
And shalt to dust return!'

Cheered by this hope, with patient mind
I'll wait Heaven's high decree,

Till the appointed period come
When death shall set us free. Amen.

NARRATOR

Amen! I felt as if a heavy hand had been pushed down over my
eyes. How could I ever see the world again? All the same, a good
time was had by all of me. Gay goes up and grim comes down. The
Puritan pepper and salt, if it looked like granite tasted like drama. It
had two sides to it. Everything in Belfast had two sides. It was so
from my first day in school.

FATHER

If I might rightly insense you into it, son. There's two kinds of
education. There's the kind you have to live to get, and there's the
kind you have to get to live. God knows, you'll get enough of the
first, just by runnin' the house and roamin' the streets! But the other
kind you'll have to have schoolin' for. Many's the good man was
lost for the want of it. I mind well when I first come to Belfast,
only about one out of every ten people could read or write their
own name. The rest didn't know 'B' from a bull's foot. The older
ones, I mean.

NARRATOR

Yes, nine men's hands went to make me write. Nine men lent their
eyes that I might read for them. Nine men's wants set me behind a
wooden desk, along with a lot of other backward Belfast boys, to
write, and read, and figure. I didn't much care for figures, but, there
were ways of getting round that. At a pinch, I could marry Miss
Arithmetic to Mr English, and all the tables would dance at the
wedding, the nine-times-seven and the seven-times-eleven – they
would all of them go on the skite, and two and two would make
six, and five into four would go forty times, and there would be no
figures left at all in the end –

Rapping of cane on desk for attention

TEACHER

Tommy Todd! Day-dreaming again! Sit up and take notice or you'll go straight to the foot of the class.

NARRATOR

That was the sad thing about life: people in this town would never let you alone. And if Mondays were bad, Sundays were worse. All week I would be full of rising spirits, but Sunday, Sunday hauled my hopes down the way that telegraph poles pull the wires down on a railway journey.

Church bell

MOTHER

Tommy Todd, are you goin' to stay upstairs all day? Are you goin' to church or aren't you? Didn't you hear the Protestant bell?

NARRATOR

It wasn't the same city at all. The streets had a pallor about them as if the blood had been drained away. And the houses looked as if they had gone round the corner on a Saturday night and come back with their faces fixed. There was an odour of goodness everywhere. Goodness was in my navy-blue suit, in my celluloid collar, in my new boots that squeaked as I walked –

MOTHER

You needn't complain. You're lucky to have a squeak. I mind when I was a girl we used to get the shoemaker to set a bit of leather in the sole to *make* them squeak. Then the whole church'd know we had a new pair of boots when we walked up the aisle.

NARRATOR

Going up to the church, the sharp little bell stopped, abruptly, as if it had bitten its tongue off. We were late.

CHOIR (Gardenmore Presbyterian Church)
I joy'd when to the house of God,
Go up, they said to me,
Jerusalem, within thy gates,
Our feet shall standing be!

NARRATOR

It was nice inside the church. Dark varnished pew, red cushion, mellow window, the blaze of the gilt-edged pulpit Bible, hushed and hallowed us all. Mrs Bittercup, in her explosive wrap of staring fox-fur, looked as if she hadn't a sound in her. Sound, on Sunday, belonged to the minister. And he was standing there in a splendid excess of silence, up to his chin in the black thunderfall of his gown with its lightning-snags of Geneva bands.

MINISTER

... And unto Adam he said, Because thou hast hearkened unto the voice of thy wife, and hast eaten of the tree, of which I commanded thee, saying, Thou shalt not eat of it: cursed is the ground for thy sake. In sorrow shalt thou eat of it all the days of thy life; thorns also and thistles shall it bring forth to thee, and thou shalt eat the herb of the field ...

NARRATOR

... Skerry Blues, King Edwards, Kerr's Pinks, British Queens, Arran Banners, Majestics ...

MOTHER

Stop whispering, Tommy!

MINISTER

… In the sweat of thy brow shalt thou eat bread, till thou return unto the ground. For dust thou art, and unto dust thou shalt return.

NARRATOR

I thought of the great mill-chimneys, those living testaments to the fall of Adam and the rise of Belfast. Of this great city that never took its smoky hat off except to God, on Sundays. The silence in church was so intense that I wanted to cough. My father put a white burning cough-sweet into my hand to keep me quiet during the prayer.

MINISTER

O God, who dost establish the work of our hands, and who satisfieth our mouth, give us, we beseech thee, these things: Give us grace – give us gear. But above all, give us *gumption*, the gumption to use them …

NARRATOR

I walked home with my eyes shut so that I could see red. It was very pleasant. 'Grace' – 'Grace'. What was it Mickey Clark called it? 'The juice of bacon.'

MOTHER

For goodness sake, Tommy, mind where you're goin'. Have you no gumption at all, knockin' into the people like that.

TOMMY

My ma's a suffragette,
She wears a big white hat,
Walkin' all around the town,
Knockin' all the people down.

MOTHER

Be quiet, will you! What'll people think? What kind of carry-on is that? Don't you know what day it is?

NARRATOR

I did indeed know what day it was. It was the longest day of the week. Every minute seemed to have mildew on it sometimes. There was nothing to do but watch the cat walking on the back wall, or read a book. And no sooner did I open a book than the Voice of Duty lighted on me like a gadfly.

MOTHER

Is that a Sunday book you're reading, Tommy? Let me see.

NARRATOR

There was God's plenty of books; great grass-grown rides of greedy reading among the dark thickets of duty. I got to be very knowing about the lives of the saints and the martyrs, particularly the sins they had been saved from and the bloody ends they had come to. Those Roman emperors had no flies on them when it came to sticky endings. Though what else, said my mother, could you expect from Rome, the oppressor of the saints. Still, there *were* some good Romans, as my father and Mr Knight allowed, when Patrick Keogh the publican died.

FATHER

A decent man, Paddy, if ever there was one. There's no knowing the good he done.

KNIGHT

One of the ould sort. It was right hand, left hand, with him all the way. There'll be a place for him up above, Roman or no Roman.

MOTHER

They could put us Protestants to shame the way they attend their church.

KNIGHT

I've known them the best of neighbours, Mrs Todd. Better maybe than some of our own.

MOTHER

Maybe it's their flyness, Mr Knight.

NARRATOR

Two little dickie-birds sittin' on the wall,
One called Peter, the other called Paul
Fly away Peter –

MOTHER

That's enough of your ould rhymes! Run out into the street and play yourself. Go on with you, now.

NARRATOR

And jagged as whins in June the watering cart would come, sprinkling the dusty street. Then we'd off with our boots and go dancing behind it, kicking against the cool prick of water and singing –

VOICE (sung by Gerard Dillon)
Fan a winnow winnow winnow
Fan a winnow daisy
Fan a winnow hi-i-addy
And away with Tommy the band-tier-o

There was some gypsies in a row,
O but they were bonny.

Some so sweet, so very very sweet
They would charm the heart of a lady-o
A lovely, blue-eyed lady-o.

NARRATOR
July brought the drums, and the drums brought the rain:
a diminuendo of rain, of all sorts, drumming down to nothing.
There was the 'plump' of rain, the 'brave drop' of rain, the 'mizzle'
or 'wee knowing' of rain, and the 'spit' of rain.

On a day of days, in July, we would move over the hills and far away
to a country cottage outside Belfast. We went in a blue and orange
cart that was slowness itself. You could tell, then, where the city
ended and the country began. There was no overspill, no straggle of
bungalows lying where they fell in their flight from the town; just
green fields. And the cottage had every modern inconvenience: an
annual bus passed the door five miles away. But it was heaven. The
duck twirled like a stick on the stream; each gay cloud was off on
its own. The corncrake at night, the cuckoo by day, the flowing
horse, the flowering bull, the smoke of flies, the ringing scythe, the
chatter of reapers, the pear tree in the garden, the pincushions of
dew – all was heaven. Apart from my enemy, the nettle, there was
only one flaw in it all.

GOSPEL SINGERS, 'Life at best is very brief'
(sung by The Ulster Singers)

Life at best is very brief,
Like the falling of a leaf,
Like the binding of a sheaf,
Be in time …

NARRATOR
Every summer the gospel tents would descend on the fields like the
Pentecostal tongues, and the reapers of souls would cut great

swathes of hymns through the standing silence of the day and night. Every breeze carried the warning sound. It was one of the banes of my life. For, just when my country day was at its tiptoppling height –

MOTHER
Tommy! Tommy! It's time you were gettin' on you. You're goin' to the gospel tent … Now you needn't be makin' faces. You're goin' and that's that.

NARRATOR
The best days, by far, were the ones I spent on the farm where there was always a boon of people and birds and beasts galore. And, once in a season, the pig-killer would arrive. Then there was pandemonium.

Uproar of pigs

NARRATOR
And afterwards there were bladders to be blown-up like balloons. I watched with fascinated horror as the big man stunned the pig and drew the knife across its throat. Then he would ask for a cup, and he would drink a salubrious draught of the blood.

BUTCHER
There's good health in it, boy: great health, if only you knowed it.

GOSPEL SINGERS (sung by The Ulster Singers)
There is power, power, wonder-working power,
In the blood of the Lamb,
There is power, power, wonder-working power
In the precious blood of the Lamb.

NARRATOR

Far, far away, the strains of the gospel song came gently on the breeze. Mystery, all of it. So much redness to redeem all this greenness. So much death to make life everlasting.

The big red drum that sounded every day across the fields seemed to repeat the dark refrain. But the little gay fife that went with it, spoke of life.

'The whins, the whins, the ould sharp whins' – that was what the drum said. The drums were warming up for the Twelfth now and I wished I could be back in Belfast to see the kingly-painted walls, and the wonderful rafts of rivering flags winding through the streets of the windfall city. There would be a bonfire in our back street that night. It would light up the roses on the wallpaper of the return room. It would flicker the picture of Robbie Burns. It would glimmer on the tallboy with its deep drawers full of treasures – even the still little Georgian mirror would go wig-wag in the glare of it. How long would it be, I reflected, before my farthing face would grow to a crown? And would I ever be able to see myself, *all* of myself? For there was no full-length mirror in our Puritan house. Such a thing would have been an abomination, a sin *in excelsis*, for it might have got too enamoured of a person. Anyway, we were an outlooking people, we Ulster folk, my father said, when he read his Bible –

FATHER

'I will lift up mine eyes unto the hills, from whence cometh my help. My help cometh from the Lord, which made heaven and earth. He will not suffer thy foot to be moved: he that keepeth thee will not slumber nor sleep.'

NARRATOR

In the nighttime, when the city clocks cleared their throats and spoke the hour, I would waken and watch the moon hurrying

through her devotions of cloud. Far below, like eternity, the tugboat
hooted to the seventh heaven of its belief.

Tugboat hooting

The river ran through the city and through my dreams like a
leading principle. Far and wild it ran, and manys a night I rescued a
beautiful princess from its angry waters by leaping from the top of
the Albert Bridge. What she would be doing on those dull
mudbanks, so late and so often, only a Belfast child would know.

CHILD SINGING (from St Comgall's)
A for apple, P for pear,
All the girls with the long yellow hair,
All the girls that I ever knew
The love I had for my lady-o,
My lady-o, my lady-o,
My lovely blue-eyed lady-o.

NARRATOR
To reach the city centre one had to cross the Albert Bridge. So my
mother always talked of going 'over town'.

MOTHER
Was I over town? I was. And what did I buy you? A wee know-
nothing with a whistle on the end of it.

NARRATOR
It was a fine evening when we both went over town. My mouth
fell open and stayed open – there was so much to gape at. The
sawmill with the lovely whine and the sawdust flying like gravy
sparks. Carts dripping with wet slummage from the distillery. Little
shops with string dangling from coloured canisters. The shining
river, fluted like a stick of celery. Kite-tails of gulls hung over the

river, and over the bridge hung dozens of people, watching a pig that had escaped from May's Fields. So it wasn't true what Mickey Clark had said, that a pig would cut its own throat when swimming.

I gazed a long time at the City Hall where Mr Jellybelly, who had a good job in the Corporation, was supposed to use his influence.

MOTHER

Aye, maybe he does, when he's not *under* the influence.

NARRATOR

Look Mother! Round the corner was a long, elegant Georgian building, a school by all appearances. 'Who knows?' said my mother —

MOTHER

If you mind your Ps and Qs you might be goin' there someday.

NARRATOR

In one corner of the lawns grazed a great brute of a building, like the gentleman that pays the rent.

MOTHER

That's the Technical School, Tommy. If you don't stick to your books and learn, you'll go there. So, take care.

NARRATOR

Outside in the roadway stood the Black Man, a statue of a Presbyterian divine who had once notably confuted the errors of Arianism. And, not a beagle's gowl away, we crossed the Falls Road. Here the Scarlet Woman reigned, and the Adversary held open court. My mother hurried me on into no-man's-land and

Smithfield, past Mr Love's shop. 'What does H–Y–G–I–E–N–E spell?' I asked. 'Come on.' She took my hand and dragged me grimly on.

MOTHER

Never you go lookin' into *that* shop, Tommy. There's nothin' but bad goes on there.

NARRATOR

Women and girls in black shawls were streaming out of the linen-mills, the girls hurrying to get home to get out again.

VOICE (sung by Gerard Dillon)
Ah, you'd easy know a doffer
When she goes down the town
With her long yellow hair
And her ringlets hanging down,
And her rubber tied before her,
And her pickers in her hand,
Ah, you'd easy know a doffer,
She'll always get a man.

Ah, she'll always get a man,
Ah, she'll always get a man,
Ah, you'd easy know a doffer,
She'll always get a man.

NARRATOR

A nightfall of newsboys was crying the papers over the city, as we went home. The purple hills stood still like hoardings at the end of the streets, and the slow sky crowded its golden colour into one last blush. And at the edge of the die-lightly day the silver pigeons wheeled, and, over all, the grey hair-lines of rain, hours long, began to fall, rippling the puddles and stippling the walls, and filling the pearly pubs, and crinkling the pavement like a cabbage leaf. No wonder that Ezekiel Knight wept over the beauty of the drowned city as he listened to my father reading from the Book.

FATHER

'... Alas, alas that great city, that was clothed in fine linen, and purple, and scarlet, and decked with gold, and precious stones, and pearls! For in one hour so great riches is come to nought.'

KNIGHT

Aye, Adam, as the flower of the field, so we perish.

FATHER

'... Alas, alas that great city, wherein were made rich all that had ships on the sea – '

KNIGHT

Say no more, say no more, Adam.

NARRATOR

Winter came. The weathercock went east, and the wind moaned and mewed in the chimney gable. My father took me to the tailor's shop at the Bridge. The tailor was a poet of sorts. He had one verse that took up half the window.

'When winter issues his decree,
And biting winds blow from the sea,
Then come with me and don with glee
A Garmoyle coat at three pounds three.'

'It's good stuff,' said the tailor, fingering the coat. 'It'll turn.' 'Turn or Burn!' said the slogan, chalked on the wall outside. Yes, even the walls of Belfast took sides. They were as full of party slogans as a moth is full of holes. 'Vote Early!' said one wall. 'Vote Often!' said the other. Orange and Green, joined in holy deadlock, ran hand-in-hand through the little streets, or played hardy knuckles with the walls.

CHILD

Holy Father, what'll I do?
I've come to confess my sins to you.
Holy Father I killed a cat.
You'll have to suffer, my child, for that.
Holy Father, what'll it be?
Forty days without any tea.
Father dear, it's far too long.
You've done, my child, a very great wrong.
But, Father dear, 'twas a Protestant cat.
Good my girl, you did right to do that.

NARRATOR

It was from children that we learned these rhymes. History was never handed *down*, it was handed up, as if from some deep kindergarten cave. It was in the bounce of a ball, the flip of a skipping rope. Our politer games we kept for drawing-rooms and grown-ups, evenings when cakes and crackers broke the ice.

CHILDREN

Down on the carpet we shall kneel
While the grass grows underfoot.
Stand up straight upon your feet
And choose the one you love so sweet.

Now we're married, life and joy,
First a girl and then a boy —

NARRATOR

I listened. I could hear my mother talking at the hall-door to Mulligan the postman.

MOTHER

You'll hardly hear yourself, with all that carry-on upstairs.

MULLIGAN

Ah sure, we're only young once, ma'am.

MOTHER

If it's a fair question, now, how many of a family have you?

MULLIGAN

Twelve. There's Mary and Malachy, Aloysius, Bridie, and then there's Maureen –

MOTHER

Lord bless us, man! That's a quare brood. However do you manage?

MULLIGAN

Ach now, between havin' and wantin' we make do.

MOTHER

Ah, it's a struggle, these times.

MULLIGAN

Well, it's like this, ma'am. You couldn't buy one of them children from me, no, not for ten thousand pound. But if you were to offer me the idea of another one, well, you could have it for tuppence.

CHILDREN

... seven years after, seven years to come,
O Geordie, Geordie, have another one.

NARRATOR

Time, that diminishes us all, has brought a new grief of children to fill the old roads and the dancing back-streets of Belfast. Still the songs live on, happy-ever-laughter.

RAGAMUFFINS

Our queen can birl her leg, birl her leg, birl her leg,
Our queen can birl her leg, birl her leg.

NARRATOR

But the old people are gone, over the hills and far away. Mrs Bittercup —

MRS BITTERCUP

The place is getting so common nowadays!

NARRATOR

Ezekiel Knight —

KNIGHT

Say no more, say no more.

NARRATOR

My mother —

MOTHER

Tell Tommy to wear a hat, matron. It'll be more respectable.

NARRATOR

My father —

FATHER

'In the morning we're like grass that groweth up: in the evening it's cut down and withered. For we are consumed by thine anger, and by thy wrath we are troubled.'

NARRATOR

They are gone, the old residenters. The mill-horn has sounded for them on the other side. But I'd give a sugar-bag of polite talk for just one nip of their bitter old Puritan tongues, one pull of their racy old pipes. Still the wind rises and the rain falls over Belfast.

And still in the dark pubs the eternal mourners,
Standing by the empty grave of their glasses,
Wait for the fulfilling word
And gaze at the ring-worm end
To which all flesh shall come.

BELFAST MAN

Have a pint, mister. It's all just a jar o' worms anyway.

NARRATOR

Up the resurrection!

VOICE

Up the rebels!

NARRATOR

Strange city, god-fearing, far-faring, devil-may-caring. I would need a gold pen as big as a gun, filled with heart's blood, to put down the rehoboams of its praise and the passion of its ways. Where are the eyes that were so true, so blue? From the window of the Return Room I see the childhood city, acres and ogres away, lying open like a monster eye, staring up at the soft sky and the wet Atlantic winds, and crying 'Weep for Polyphemus, and the once-was.'

By the waters
The ever and nevering waters of
Lagan I sat down and wept.
I wept with one eye at a time
(Being parsimonious), once for life
And once for joy.
First a girl and then a boy.
After life's fitful fever
We weep well.

My Lagan Love

sung by Gerard Dillon

Where Lagan stream sings lullaby
There dwells a lily fair
The dew of eve is in her eye
The night is on her hair
And like a love-sick lennan-shee
She has my heart in thrall
No life I own nor liberty
For love is lord of all.

Sam Hanna Bell at the production desk. This drawing – by Bell's friend
Rowel Friers – is dated 20 October 1955. It was probably designed for
local newspapers or a regional edition of the *Radio Times* –
advance publicity for *The Return Room*.

ANNOUNCER

The Return Room was written and narrated by W.R. Rodgers.
The programme was produced by Sam Hanna Bell in the Northern
Ireland studios of the BBC.

The part of the mother was played by Ann Maguire and the father
by William Hunter with Elizabeth Begley, James Mageean and
James Devlin. Others taking part were Catherine Gibson, Charles
Witherspoon, James Boyce, John McBride, James McCrudden,
Marilyn Smyth, Denis Maguire, Billy McGuigan and William
McKay Kenny.